The Story of
The Birth of Jesus

By Rev. JUDE WINKLER, OFM Conv.

KT-452-520

Imprimi Potest: Daniel Pietrzak, OFM Conv., Minister Provincial of St. Anthony of Padua Province (USA)
Nihil Obstat: James T. O'Connor, S.T.D., Censor Librorum
Imprimatur: Patrick J. Sheridan, Vicar General, Archdiocese of New York

CPSIA   February 2023   10 9 8 7 6 5   L/P

© 1989 by CATHOLIC BOOK PUBLISHING CORP., Totowa, NJ
Printed in China   ISBN 978-0-89942-960-1
www.catholicbookpublishing.com

GOD SENDS HIS MESSENGER TO MARY

GOD loves the people of Israel in a very special way. He promised that He would always be with them to deliver them from the hands of their enemies. He also promised to send them one who would rule over them in His name.

The people eagerly awaited the birth of this promised one. They called Him the Messiah, and they expected Him to be a great King and a powerful warrior. God, though, had a different plan.

His Messiah would be born as a poor and simple one—for this Messiah would conquer evil not with great armies but with the greatness of His love.

And so it was that God sent the angel Gabriel, His messenger, to a young woman named Mary. Mary was betrothed to a man named Joseph, but they had not yet begun to live together. Thus, she was still a virgin.

The angel greeted Mary saying, "Hail Mary, full of grace! The Lord is with you." Mary was confused as to what this greeting meant, but Gabriel reassured her that she had found favor with God. He told her, "You will conceive and bear a son, and you shall name Him Jesus." He then told her how great that son would be.

Mary did not understand how she could have this child for she was still a virgin. But the angel said, "The Holy Spirit will come upon you and the power of the Most High will overshadow you. Therefore the child to be born will be called holy, the Son of God." The angel also said that Elizabeth, her cousin, was pregnant even though she was very old, for nothing was impossible for God.

Mary then answered, "Behold, I am the hand-maid of the Lord. May it be done to me according to your word."

4

MARY VISITS ELIZABETH

BY saying yes to the Lord's call, Mary was placing herself in great danger. She was engaged to Joseph, and he could have accused her of being unfaithful. He could have even had her put to death. But Mary trusted in the Lord.

Joseph, being a good man, decided that he would not have Mary punished in public. Instead, he would send her away quietly. But an angel visited him in a dream that night and explained to him that Mary had not been unfaithful. She was pregnant by the Holy Spirit. Joseph cared for Mary and took her to his home.

Mary was not worried about her own problems. She realized that her cousin, Elizabeth, was very old and that she would need her help. So Mary traveled in haste to the hill country of Judea to be with Elizabeth.

As soon as Elizabeth heard Mary's voice, she knew something very special had happened. The baby in her womb jumped for joy, and Elizabeth was filled with the Holy Spirit.

Elizabeth greeted Mary saying, "Most blessed are you among women, and blessed is the fruit of your womb." She asked how the mother of her Lord would come to visit her for she felt unworthy of so great an honor.

THE BIRTH OF JOHN THE BAPTIST

ELIZABETH also told Mary that she was sure Mary was blessed because she had trusted in what God had said to her through the angel.

Mary was filled with joy over all that had happened to her, and she answered Elizabeth by singing a song of praise to the Lord. She still found it difficult to believe that the Lord had chosen her, a weak and humble person, and had not chosen someone who was rich and powerful.

Mary stayed with her cousin Elizabeth for three months. At the end of that time, Elizabeth gave birth to a fine baby. On the eighth day after the baby was born, Elizabeth and Zechariah took him to be circumcised. When the elders asked her what name he was to be given, she said "John." The elders were confused for usually the child would be named after the father or grandfather. There was no one in their family named John.

They asked Zechariah what name the boy should be given. Now Zechariah had not been able to speak since the angel had spoken to him in the Temple to tell him about the future birth of his son. So Zechariah took a tablet and wrote the name John. At that very moment, he was healed and could once again speak. He praised the Lord for all the wonders He had worked.

JOSEPH AND MARY TRAVEL
TO BETHLEHEM

ABOUT this time, the Roman emperor called for a census. He wanted to find out how many people there were in his empire so that he could know how much they should pay him in taxes. Each man was to go back to the city of his birth with his whole family and register there.

So Joseph took Mary and they traveled from Nazareth where they were living to Bethlehem, the city of David. Joseph was a descendant of the great King David. Mary was in her ninth month, and it was a very difficult trip for her.

NO ROOM IN THE INN

THERE were so many people traveling that when Joseph and Mary looked for a place to spend the night, there was no room for them in the inn. They went from house to house, but no one had a place for them to stay.

Finally, one family took pity on them. There was no room for Joseph and Mary in their house, but they told them that they could stay in their stable. This stable was a cave where their animals would stay when the weather was cold, and Joseph and Mary would at least be warm there.

MARY GIVES BIRTH TO JESUS

JOSEPH took Mary to that cave outside of Bethlehem. They took some clean straw and made a bed. They made themselves as comfortable as possible.

It was not their home, but the great love and goodness that Joseph and Mary had was enough for them.

Mary's time came, and she gave birth to a son whom they would name Jesus, a name which means that Yahweh saves. This fulfilled all that the angel Gabriel had told Mary.

Mary took her baby son and wrapped Him in swaddling clothes, a kind of blanket. She and Joseph cleaned out one of the mangers, the place where the farmers would put hay for the animals. They put fresh straw in the manger and used it as a crib for their baby.

This was not the way the people believed that the Messiah would be born. They expected their king to be born in a palace and not in a stable.

Joseph gathered the animals and brought them close around the mother and child so that they would provide some warmth during the night. It seemed as if the animals realized what was happening and were praising the Lord.

THE ANGELS APPEAR TO THE SHEPHERDS

NEARBY there were some shepherds watching over their flocks. Shepherds in those days were not very nice persons. People did not trust them because they were afraid that the shepherds would rob something. For that reason, shepherds usually lived outside the cities, and people did not want to have them around.

Yet the very first people to whom the news of Jesus' birth was announced were these shepherds. An angel appeared to them, and all of a sudden they were surrounded by great lights. They were very frightened.

The angel reassured them and told them, "Do not be afraid; for behold, I proclaim to you good news of great joy that will be for all the people. For today in the city of David a savior has been born for you who is Messiah and Lord."

The angel then told the shepherds what they would see. He said that the child would be wrapped in swaddling clothes and lying in a manger. Suddenly there was a large number of angels singing and praising the Lord. The angels sang out,

"Glory to God in the highest
and on earth peace to people of good will."

THE SHEPHERDS GO TO WORSHIP
THE BABY

SUDDENLY, the angels vanished. The shepherds said, "Let us go to Bethlehem to see this thing which the Lord has made known to us."

They traveled in haste to Bethlehem to see the things that the angel had spoken of. When they arrived, they found everything just as the angel had promised. There before them was the baby wrapped in swaddling clothes and lying in a manger. They told Mary and Joseph everything that had happened to them that night.

THE SHEPHERDS PRAISE THE LORD

ALL the people who heard about what had happened to the shepherds, of how the angels had appeared and announced this great news to them, were filled with wonder. Mary kept all these things in her heart. She often wondered what all this meant.

After the shepherds had seen the babe and had given their gifts to Him and His parents, they went on their way. They returned to the fields where they were tending their sheep.

All the way home they kept talking among themselves about the wonders that they had seen that night. They praised the Lord because of all that He had done and especially because He had revealed these great things to them.

JESUS IS TAKEN TO THE TEMPLE

ON the eighth day after Jesus was born, Joseph and Mary took their baby to be circumcised. They gave Him the name Jesus, the name that the angel Gabriel had spoken to Mary.

Then, when it was time for Mary to be purified, they went up to the Temple in Jerusalem. Mary and Joseph brought along two turtle doves as an offering to the Lord. This was the offering that was to be made by people who were too poor to make a larger offering. They also brought along their baby, Jesus, who was now a little more than a month old.

There was an old man named Simeon in the Temple. The Holy Spirit had promised Simeon that he would not die until he saw the promised one of the Lord. As soon as he saw Jesus, Simeon knew that this baby was the Messiah.

Simeon thanked the Lord because He had kept His promise. He also told Mary that Jesus would be a reason for joy for many in Israel but that others would reject Him.

There was also an elderly woman worshiping in the Temple that day. This woman, Anna, was 84 years old. She came forward at that very moment and gave thanks to God for the child. She told everyone in Jerusalem about Him.

THE MAGI TRAVEL TO JERUSALEM

IN those days, there were people who would study the stars in order to find out what was going to happen in the future. One of the names given to these people was Magi. Many of them lived in the countries to the east of Israel.

Three of these Magi were looking at the skies when suddenly they saw a new star. They studied the star and realized that it was a sign that a new King had been born to the Jews.

The Magi set out from their own country in the east in order to meet that new King. They traveled with their servants and camels and the gifts that they were bringing to the baby.

This was a very dangerous trip, but the Magi knew that it was important for them to take the risk. They knew that this star was the sign of a most important King.

When the Magi arrived in Jerusalem, they looked around for information about the baby. They went up to many people and said, "Where is the newborn King of the Jews? We saw His star at its rising and have come to do Him homage." They were sure that everyone would know about Him, but it just was not so. No one whom they asked had heard anything about a newborn King.

THE MAGI MEET KING HEROD

SOON a report about these three Magi reached King Herod, the king of the Jews. He was a very evil man and had killed many people because he had thought that they wanted to be king. When he heard that the Magi were speaking about a newborn King, he became frightened.

King Herod called the chief priests and the scribes together and asked them about the promised Messiah. He wanted to know where this Messiah would be born.

The priests and scribes studied the question and then told the king that the prophets had spoken about how the Messiah would be born in Bethlehem, the city of David. Bethlehem was called the city of David because the great king of Israel had been born there.

King Herod then called the Magi in to talk with them in secret. He asked them when they had first seen the star and many other things. When they had answered all of his questions, he sent them away. He told them to go to Bethlehem so that they could find the child. When they had found Him, they were to send word to King Herod for he told them that he wanted to go and pay his respects to the child. However, he really wanted to kill Him.

22

THE MAGI WORSHIP THE CHILD

A S soon as the Magi set out, they once again saw the star. It was only about five miles from Jerusalem to Bethlehem, so the Magi were able to travel there in a short time.

When they arrived in Bethlehem, they saw that the star had stopped over a cave just outside the city. They went there and found Joseph, Mary, and the Baby Jesus.

The Magi immediately entered the stable and fell down on their knees. They honored the child and brought out the gifts that they had brought Him from their homeland. They brought Him gifts of gold, frankincense, and myrrh.

It is said that there was a special meaning to these gifts, a meaning that even the Magi may not have realized when they chose them.

Gold was a gift that someone would give to a king. It is a sign of the fact that Jesus is the King of the Jews and the King of all kings. Frankincense is a type of incense. One would normally burn it as an offering to God. It was a sign of the hidden fact that Jesus is the only Son of God. Finally, myrrh is an ointment that one would use when someone was being buried. It pointed to the way that Jesus would free us from our sins, through His death and resurrection.

THE FLIGHT INTO EGYPT

THE Magi were going to go back to Jerusalem to tell King Herod about the child, but an angel appeared to them in a dream and told them to go back a different way.

When they had left, this angel spoke to Joseph in a dream as well. He warned him that King Herod was seeking to harm the child. The angel told Joseph to take Jesus and His mother and to flee to Egypt.

Joseph woke up Mary and they gathered together everything that they had and set out for Egypt with the Baby Jesus that very night. There the baby would be safe from the evil King Herod. What they did also fulfilled what one of the prophets had said long ago, "Out of Egypt I called my son."

King Herod waited for the Magi to return back to him and give him a report about the child, but it soon became clear that they were not going to come back. He sent out his soldiers with the order that they were to kill all the baby boys who lived anywhere around Bethlehem who were two years old or younger.

The soldiers went throughout the town and the surrounding countryside and killed every small baby boy they found. They showed no mercy in spite of the cries of the mothers.

THE RETURN TO NAZARETH

A SHORT time later Joseph and Mary heard the report that the evil King Herod had died. They knew it would now be safe for them to leave their refuge in Egypt and take their baby back to their home.

When Joseph and Mary set out, they heard that Herod's son, Archelaus, was now ruling in Jerusalem. They also heard that he was even a worse man than his father.

Joseph and Mary knew that their baby would be in great danger if they went back to Bethlehem. Therefore, they did not want to return there.

Joseph and Mary decided that they would travel back to Nazareth, the city where they had been living before the census. There they would certainly be safe from everything that might harm them.

And so Joseph and Mary took their child Jesus and made the long journey back to the village of Nazareth.

When they arrived there, Joseph set up a house for his family. He had always been a carpenter, and now he was able to have a small shop in which he could do his work and earn a living for his family.

JESUS GROWS IN GRACE AND WISDOM

JESUS grew up big and strong, but He also grew in grace and wisdom. In so many ways He was like all the other boys of the village. Yet there was something special about Him.

Mary sewed His clothes, prepared His food, and watched over Him. She saw how He helped her around the house and her husband in the carpenter shop. He looked so normal.

And yet she knew He was special for she had received the message from the angel. This must have been very confusing for Mary. But she kept praying, and she placed her trust in the Lord.

JESUS HELPS IN THE CARPENTER SHOP

L IKE the other children of His time, Jesus probably attended school at the synagogue. There He would learn a little about reading and writing, geography and history, all by reading the stories of the Bible.

Jesus would also have learned some important lessons at home. Joseph was a carpenter, and he probably taught Jesus all about the work that he did.

Jesus probably also learned much from Mary His mother. She showed Him how to trust in the Lord, for she had done this in her own life.

JESUS IS LOST IN THE TEMPLE

JOSEPH and Mary were very good Jews, and each year they would travel up to Jerusalem for the great feast of Passover. When Jesus was twelve years old, the age at which a Jewish boy became a man, they took Him up with them.

After the feast, Joseph and Mary set out to return to Nazareth. They looked around for Jesus, but they could not find Him. At first they thought He was in another part of the camp. But when they came to rest that evening and still did not find Him, they realized He was lost.

Joseph and Mary returned to Jerusalem and looked for Jesus for three days. They went up to the Temple and searched for Him there.

His parents were most surprised when they found Jesus sitting in the Temple and speaking with the elders. He was listening to their teaching and asking them questions.

Mary went up to Jesus and asked Him, "Son, why have You done this to us? Your father and I have been looking for You."

Jesus answered her, "Why were you looking for Me? Did you not know that I must be in My Father's house?" He then returned with Mary and Joseph and stayed in Nazareth until the day that He began His preaching.

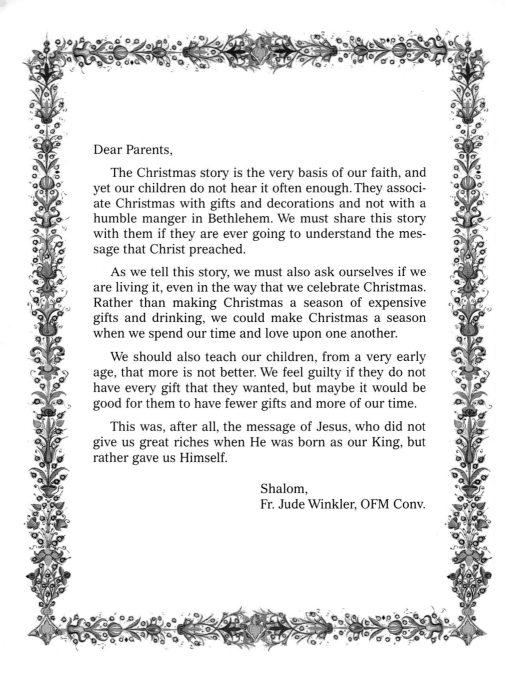

Dear Parents,

The Christmas story is the very basis of our faith, and yet our children do not hear it often enough. They associate Christmas with gifts and decorations and not with a humble manger in Bethlehem. We must share this story with them if they are ever going to understand the message that Christ preached.

As we tell this story, we must also ask ourselves if we are living it, even in the way that we celebrate Christmas. Rather than making Christmas a season of expensive gifts and drinking, we could make Christmas a season when we spend our time and love upon one another.

We should also teach our children, from a very early age, that more is not better. We feel guilty if they do not have every gift that they wanted, but maybe it would be good for them to have fewer gifts and more of our time.

This was, after all, the message of Jesus, who did not give us great riches when He was born as our King, but rather gave us Himself.

Shalom,
Fr. Jude Winkler, OFM Conv.